GOD LOVES MY PRAYERS

Prayers and Classic Rhymes for Children

Written by

Adorae Younge

GOD LOVES MY PRAYERS

Copyright © Adorae Younge, 2025

All rights reserved. No part of this book may be reproduced, stored in a retrieval system, or transmitted in any form or by any means, electronic, mechanical, photocopying, recording, or otherwise, without the prior written permission of the publisher, except for brief quotations in reviews or articles.

Copyright owner.

Email **turningmirror@outlook.com**

Book cover design, illustrations, layout, formatting & editing by Christian Book Editor Ltd.

Email: cbe@christianbookeditor.uk

"Prayer for Protection" by James Dillet Freeman. Copyright © 1941 by Unity School of Christianity. Used with permission.

Scripture quotations are taken from the King James Version (KJV) of the Bible. Public domain.

Classic prayers included in this book are in the public domain and used with gratitude.

All other original prayers, rhymes, and writings © 2025 by Adorae Younge.

This book includes Bible verses from the Holy Bible, with quotations taken from their respective translations and used in accordance with their copyright policies.

The following notices apply:

NIV: The New International Version (NIV) is copyrighted by the International Bible Society. Used by permission. All rights reserved.

KJV: The Holy Bible, King James Version (KJV), is in the public domain. All rights reserved.

CONTENTS PAGE

Introduction..1

God's Big Words.. 14

Divine Order 18

Morning Prayers 22

Prayers of Thanks... 28

Family and Friends... 36

Daily Living.. 44

Healing and Comfort..56

Bible Prayers 63

Evening and Bedtime 72

ACKNOWLEDGEMENTS

First and foremost, I thank You, Almighty God, for Your inspiration.

I extend heartfelt thanks to my dear, sweet mother, Elaine Younge, now 105 years old, who taught me the classic prayers of childhood, the very ones that she herself recited as a little girl in the 1920s.

I have fond memories of my childhood when every day, morning, noon, and night, she prayed with me. These prayers became more than words spoken; they became a rhythm of life, filled with comfort, joy, and God's holy presence.

This book is dedicated in part to her faithful example, which has shaped my own walk with God and inspired me to pass these prayers on to future generations of little ones.

DEDICATION

To the youngest children of God, may these prayers guide your steps and remind you that wherever you are, God is.

"Let the little children come to me, and do not hinder them, for the kingdom of heaven belongs to such as these" (Matthew 19:14).

INTRODUCTION

Prayer is talking with God

The same way you talk to your family and friends is the same way you can talk to God about anything.

One day, Jesus's disciples came to Him and said, *"Lord, teach us to pray."*

They wanted to know how to speak to God the way Jesus did. So, Jesus taught them a very special prayer that we call **<u>The Lord's Prayer.</u>**

This prayer reminds us that God is our Father in heaven, who loves us so dearly. He provides for us; He forgives us, and He helps us every day.

When you pray, you can thank God for the good things in your life. You can ask Him to help you when you are afraid or sad. You can also pray for the people and animals you love. God always listens.

Prayer is a way to remember that you are never alone. Whether you are at school, at home, at the park, or tucked up in bed, God is always near and cares for you.

This little book will help you learn some special prayers, old and new, that children have prayed for many years. You can say them by yourself, with your family, or even whisper them quietly in your heart.

Every prayer is a way of saying:

"Thank You, Lord. I love You, and I know You love me too."

Why do some people close their eyes when they pray?

When we pray, some people close their eyes. This isn't because God can only hear us that way. We close our eyes to help us think about God instead of being distracted by everything around us.

Why do some people put their hands together when we pray?

Some people put their hands together when they pray, not because they have to, but because it helps them stay still and quiet while talking to God.

Why do some people kneel down when they pray?

There are many ways to pray. We can do that by standing, sitting, kneeling, or even lying down in bed. The most important thing is not how we look, but that we open our hearts to God, who loves to hear us.

And sometimes, we don't even need to use words. God hears us if we pray quietly in our hearts, because He knows our thoughts and loves to listen.

What Does "Amen" Mean?

When we finish a prayer, we often say **"Amen"**.

"Amen" is a special word that means **"Yes, Lord, I agree"** or **"Let it be so"**.

It's like putting a seal at the end of your prayer to show that you believe what you just said and you are trusting God to hear it.

So, when you say **"Amen"**, you're saying, *"Yes, God, this is my prayer, and I know You are listening"*.

Joy

Everlasting

Saviour

Unfailing

Shepherd

J: Joy—Jesus gives us joy in our hearts.
E: Everlasting—His love never ends.
S: Saviour—Jesus saves us and cares for us.
U: Unfailing—He never leaves us, no matter what.
S: Shepherd—Jesus guides us like a good shepherd.

JESUS: Love & Kindness

- **J: Joyful Friend**—Jesus is always happy to be with us.
- **E: Encourager**—He helps us keep going.
- **S: Strong**—Jesus is powerful and protects us.
- **U: Unconditional Love**—He loves us no matter what.
- **S: Servant**—Jesus showed kindness by serving others.

JESUS: Prayer & Faith

- **J: Just**—Jesus is fair and good.
- **E: Eternal**—He lives forever.
- **S: Saviour**—He rescues us from sin.
- **U: Understanding**—Jesus knows how we feel.
- **S: Son of God**—That's who He is!

JESUS: Friendship & Care

- **J: Joy... giver**—He fills our hearts with happiness.
- **E: Example**—Jesus shows us how to live.
- **S: Safe**—We are safe with Him.
- **U: Unchanging**—Jesus is the same yesterday, today, and forever.
- **S: Supporter**—He is always by our side.

"The name of the Lord is a strong tower; the righteous run to it and are safe."

– Proverbs 18:10

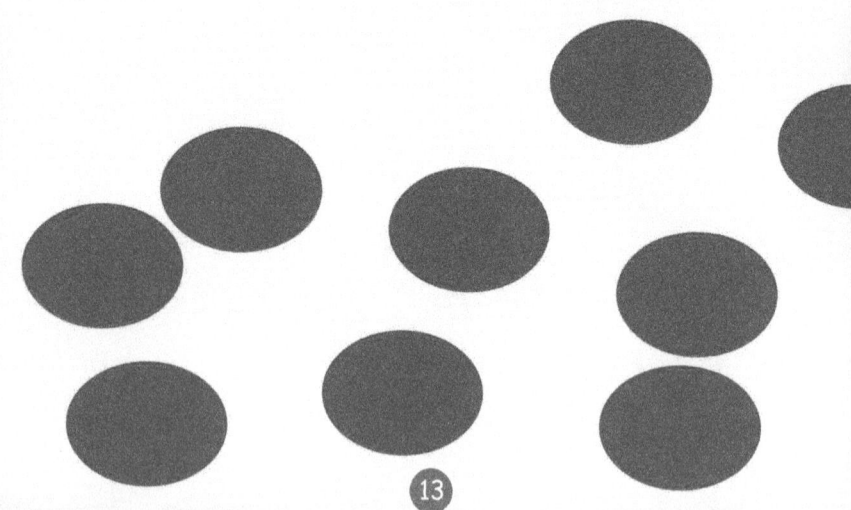

GOD'S BIG WORDS

Sometimes, we use big words to describe how amazing God is. These words help us understand Him better.

- **Omniscient**
  (sounds like OM-NEE-SEE-ENT) **means God knows everything.**

- **Omnipresent**
  (sounds like OM-NEE-PRES-ENT) **means God is everywhere.**

- **Omnipotent**
  (sounds like OM-NEE-PO-TENT) **means God is all-powerful.**

God is greater than we can imagine, and He loves us very much.

A Prayer About God's Big Words

Dear God,
Thank You that You know everything,
are always with me,
and have the power to do all things.
Help me to trust You every day,
because You are so great
and You love me so much.
Amen.

God's Big Words in Rhymes

- **Omniscient (All-Knowing)**
  God knows the things I do and say.
  He knows my thoughts both night and day.
  He understands what's in my heart,
  From His great wisdom, I can't part.
- **Omnipresent (Always With Us)**
  Wherever I go, both far and near,
  God is beside me, always here.
  At home, at school, or when I play,
  His love is with me every day.
- **Omnipotent (All-Powerful)**
  God is strong, His power is great,
  He rules the world He did create.
  He holds me safe in all I do,
  There's nothing God cannot see through.

What Is Divine Order?

Divine is another big word.

It is said like (DEE-VINE)

The word **Divine** means something that comes from **God**.

It is holy, pure, and perfect just like Him.

When we say *Divine Love*, it means the kind of love that comes from God.
When we say *Divine Order*, it means the way God has made everything to work together in the right way.

So "Divine" is a special word that reminds us: *this is from God, and it is good.*

Divine means God has made the world in a special way. Everything has its right place and time. This is called Divine Order.

Think about the sun; it always rises in the morning and sets at night. Flowers open in the day and close when it's dark. Seasons follow one after another: spring, summer, autumn, and winter.

In the same way, God has a divine plan for our lives. When we listen, trust, and follow Him, we are part of His Divine Order. That means He guides us to the right place at the right time.

A Prayer About Divine Order

Dear God,
Thank You for making the world in such a beautiful way.
Help me to walk in Your order every day.
Guide my steps,
Show me Your plan,
And help me trust You,
Because You know what is best for me.
Amen.

Divine Order (Short Rhyme)

God made the sun to shine so bright,
The moon to glow with gentle light.
He guides my steps in all I do,
His perfect plan will see me through.

Morning Prayer

Good morning, Lord, I start my day,
Please guide my steps in every way.
Help me be gentle, kind, and true,
In all I think, say, and do.

Good Morning

Lord, in the morning I start each day,
By taking a moment to stop and pray.
I thank You, God, for keeping me through,
And ask for blessings in all I do.

Gentle Jesus, Meek and Mild (Charles Wesley, 1742)

Original
Gentle Jesus, meek and mild,
Look upon a little child;
Pity my simplicity,
Suffer me to come to Thee.

Adaptation
Gentle Jesus, kind and true,
I give my little heart to You.
Guide me, bless me, day by day,
Help me walk in Your way.

The Lord's Prayer (KJV)

Our Father which art in heaven,
Hallowed be Thy name.
Thy kingdom come.
Thy will be done, in earth, as it is in heaven.
Give us this day our daily bread.
And forgive us our debts,
As we forgive our debtors.
And lead us not into temptation,
But deliver us from evil:
For Thine is the kingdom,
And the power, and the glory,
For ever. Amen.

"I will give thanks to You, Lord, with all my heart."

– Psalm 9:1

Thank You Prayer

Thank You for the world so sweet,
Thank You for the food we eat,
Thank You for the birds that sing,
Thank You, God, for everything.

Thank You for the World (Original)

Thank You, Lord, for sky so blue,
For grass beneath and sunshine too.
For flowers bright and trees that grow,
And all the love You daily show.

All Things Bright and Beautiful (Cecil Frances Alexander, 1848)

Original refrain
All things bright and beautiful,
All creatures great and small,
All things wise and wonderful:
The Lord God made them all.

Adaptation
Lord, You made each bird that sings,
And every tiny, lovely thing.
Thank You for the world so fair,
And for the love You always share.

Thanksgiving Prayer

Thank You, Lord, for all I see,
For home and love and family.
For food to eat and clothes to wear,
For all Your blessings everywhere.

Thanksgiving for Creation

Thank You, Lord, for earth and sky,
For soaring birds that sing and fly.
For shining sun and gentle rain,
For all the beauty You sustain.

Prayer of Thanks for Animals and Creation

Thank You, Lord, for creatures near,
For pets I love and those I cheer.
For mountains tall and oceans wide,
Your wondrous works on every side.

"Love one another as I have loved you."

– John 13:34

Prayer for Family

Bless my family, Lord, I pray,
Keep them safe both night and day.
Fill our hearts with love so true,
And draw us close, dear Lord, to You.

Jesus, Friend of Little Children

Jesus, Friend of little children,
Be a Friend to me;
Take my hand and ever keep me,
Close to Thee.

God Bless Mummy, Daddy Too (Traditional)

God bless Mummy, Daddy too,
Bless my sister, brother too;
All the family, everyone,
God bless us all beneath the sun.

God bless my family

God bless family, near and far,
You know each one just who they are.
Hold them gently, keep them near,
Show them love throughout the year.

Prayer for Friends

Thank You, Lord, for friends I know,
For games we play and seeds we sow.
Help me share and always care,
To show Your love is everywhere.

God, Make My Life a Little Light (children's hymn... prayer)

God, make my life a little light,
Within the world to glow;
A little flame that burneth bright,
Wherever I may go.

Jesus, Friend of Little Children

Jesus, Friend of little children,
Be a Friend to me.

A Prayer for God's Protection

Many Christians have prayed for God's **light, love, and care** to surround them every day. This is one of the most loved prayers, written by James Dillet Freeman in 1941.
(I have included it here with permission from Unity).

The Prayer for Protection (Original)

The light of God surrounds me;
The love of God enfolds me;
The power of God protects me;
The presence of God watches over me.
Wherever I am, God is!

Protection Prayers for Children (New Versions)

1. Simple Bedtime Rhyme

God's light is shining all around,
His love is near, it can be found.
His power keeps me safe and strong,
I know He's with me all night long.

2. Short Prose Prayer

Dear God, thank You for surrounding me with Your light.
Thank You that Your love is always with me,
Your strength keeps me safe,
And Your presence never leaves me.
Amen.

3. Playful Daytime Rhyme

God's love above, below, beside,
Goes with me on each step and ride.
His light and care are always near,
To guide my way and calm my fear.

Original verses added by Adorae

God is my light when skies are grey,
He keeps me safe at work and play.
God is my song, my joy, my cheer,
I know His love is always near.

God is my strength when I am weak,
He gives me courage when I speak.
God is my shelter, strong and true,
His endless love will see me through.

Short Version (For Younger Children)

God is my help both night and day,
He keeps me safe at work and play.
God is my friend, so kind and true,
His love will always see me through.

Prayer for School

Bless my teachers, Lord, today,
Help me listen, learn, and obey.
Give me wisdom, help me grow,
And teach me all I need to know.

School Prayers for Children

Morning School Prayer

Dear Lord, bless my school today,
In all I think and do and say.
Help me to learn and play with care,
And show Your love is always there.

Prayer Before Lessons

"O God, who gives us light and truth,
Bless all the work we do.
Help us to learn and to be kind,
And keep us close to You."

Prayer for Teachers and Friends

"Bless my teachers, kind and true,
Guide them in the work they do.
Bless my classmates, one and all,
Keep us safe at work and play and call."

End of School Day Prayer

"Thank You, Lord, for school today,
For work and fun and time to play.
Bless my friends and keep us near,
Till we return tomorrow here."

Prayer of Forgiveness

If I have done a hurtful thing,
Please wash me clean, O Christ my King.
Forgive my sins and make me new,
So I may walk each day with You.

Prayer for Others in Need

Bless the poor, the weak, the small,
Show Your mercy to them all.
Help me share in word and deed,
To love my neighbour when in need.

"Cast all your cares on Him, because He cares for you."

– 1 Peter 5:7

Healing Prayer for Myself

Dear Jesus, make the hurting go,
Please heal me fast and help me grow.
Bring comfort, peace, and strength today,
And chase my every pain away.

Healing Prayer for Others

Dear Jesus, bless my loved ones dear,
Bring them comfort, hold them near.
Heal their bodies, make them strong,
And fill their hearts with joy and song.

When I Feel Afraid

Dear Jesus, when the dark feels near,
Please take away my every fear.
Hold me close and make me strong,
For in Your arms I do belong.

Jesus Loves Me
(Anna Bartlett Warner, 1860)

Original (first verse)
Jesus loves me—this I know,
For the Bible tells me so;
Little ones to Him belong,
They are weak, but He is strong.

Adaptation
Jesus loves me, this I know,
He will never let me go.
I am safe within His care,
Every moment, everywhere.

The Prayer of Faith
(Hannah More Kohaus)

Original
God is my help in every need;
God does my every hunger feed;
God walks beside me, guides my way
Through every moment of the day.

I now am wise, I now am true,
Patient, kind, and loving too.
All things I am, can do, and be
Through Christ, the Truth that is in me.

God is my health, I can't be sick;
God is my strength, unfailing, quick;
God is my all; I know no fear,
Since God and love and Truth are here.

Adaptation (Child... Friendly)
God is my helper every day,
He listens when I stop to pray.
He walks beside me all the way,
And keeps me safe in work and play.

God helps me learn to love and share,
To show His kindness everywhere.
With Jesus' truth to guide me through,
There's nothing He cannot help me do.

God makes me strong, I will not fear,
For He is always, always near.
His love and truth forever stay,
And guide me through my night and day.

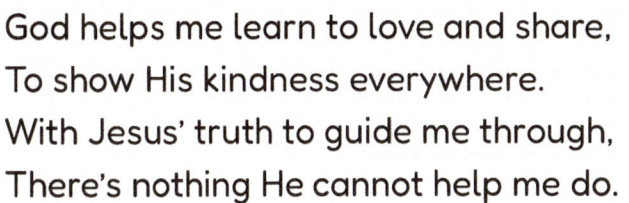

"The Lord is near to all who call on Him."

– Psalm 145:18

BIBLE PRAYERS

Psalm 23 (KJV)

The Lord is my shepherd; I shall not want.
He maketh me to lie down in green pastures:
He leadeth me beside the still waters.
He restoreth my soul:
He leadeth me in the paths of righteousness for His name's sake.
Yea, though I walk through the valley of the shadow of death,
I will fear no evil: for Thou art with me;
Thy rod and Thy staff they comfort me.
Thou preparest a table before me in the presence of mine enemies:
Thou anointest my head with oil; my cup runneth over.
Surely goodness and mercy shall follow me all the days of my life:
And I will dwell in the house of the Lord for ever.

Matthew 19:14 (Jesus' Words)

Original **(KJV)**
But Jesus said,
*Suffer little children, and forbid them not,
to come unto me:
for of such is the kingdom of heaven.*

Adaptation
Jesus said, "Let children come,
Each and every little one.
Heaven's kingdom is their place,
Held forever by God's grace."

THE LORD'S PRAYER

Our Father which art in heaven,

Hallowed be Thy name.

Thy kingdom come.

Thy will be done, in earth, as it is in heaven.

Give us this day our daily bread.

And forgive us our debts,

As we forgive our debtors.

And lead us not into temptation,

But deliver us from evil:

For Thine is the kingdom,

And the power, and the glory,

For ever and ever. Amen.

(Luke 11:1–4; Matthew 6:9–13)

"Lord, teach us to pray."

– Luke 11:1

What the Lord's Prayer Means

Our Father which art in heaven,
God is our loving Father, and He lives in heaven.

Hallowed be Thy name.
God's name is holy and special. We honour and respect Him.

Thy kingdom come.
We ask God to bring His love, peace, and goodness into the world.

Thy will be done, in earth, as it is in heaven.
We want to do what God wants, just like the angels do in heaven.

Give us this day our daily bread.
God, please give us what we need each day—food, clothes, and care.

And forgive us our debts, as we forgive our debtors.
Please forgive us when we do wrong, and help us to forgive others as well.

And lead us not into temptation, but deliver us from evil.
Keep us away from wrong choices, and protect us from harm.

For Thine is the kingdom, and the power, and the glory, for ever. Amen.
Everything belongs to You, God. You are powerful and wonderful forever!

"When I lie down, I will sleep in peace, for You alone, Lord, make me dwell in safety."

– Psalm 4:8

EVENING AND BEDTIME

Evening Prayer

As evening falls and stars appear,
I know, O Lord, that You are near.
Thank You for the blessings from today,
Please keep me safe in every way.

Jesus, Tender Shepherd, Hear Me
(Mary Lundie Duncan, 1839)

Original
Jesus, tender Shepherd, hear me,
Bless Thy little lamb tonight;
Through the darkness be Thou near me,
Keep me safe till morning light.

Adaptation
Jesus, Shepherd kind and near,
Keep me safe, remove my fear.
Through the night watch over me,
Till the morning light I see.

Glory to Thee, My God, This Night (Thomas Ken, 1692)

Original
Glory to Thee, my God, this night,
For all the blessings of the light;
Keep me, O keep me, King of kings,
Beneath Thine own almighty wings.

Adaptation
Thank You, Lord, for light today,
For fun and work and time to play.
Now I rest beneath Your care,
Knowing You are always there.

Father, We Thank Thee for the Night
(Traditional, 19th century)

Father, we thank Thee for the night,
And for the pleasant morning light;
For rest and food and loving care,
And all that makes the day so fair.

Now I Lay Me Down to Sleep (Traditional, 18th century)

Original
Now I lay me down to sleep,
I pray the Lord my soul to keep;
If I should die before I wake,
I pray the Lord my soul to take.

Adaptation
Now I lay me down to rest,
I know, dear Lord, that I am blessed.
Keep me safe all through the night,
And wake me with the morning light.

Closing Blessing Prayer

Dear Lord, please bless each child today,
Guide their steps along the way.
Keep them safe through every part,
And hold them closely to Your heart.

Why do some people say in the name of Jesus?

Sometimes, we end prayers by saying, *In the name of Jesus.*

This means we are praying with Jesus as our Friend and Helper. God listens because Jesus loves us and brings us close to Him.

What Does "God Bless You" Mean?

When you say "God bless you" to someone, you are giving them one of the most powerful prayers in the world.

Why? Because if God blesses you, you have everything you need! His blessing means love, joy, peace, safety, and care.

It's like asking God to wrap that person in His kindness and goodness.

So, when you say *"God bless you"* to your family, friends, or anyone you meet, you are giving them a beautiful gift from God's heart.

A Special Blessing for You

May God's continued and richest blessings be with you.

Why do I say this? Because when God blesses you, you have everything you need. His blessing means His love is with you, His peace fills your heart, and His goodness surrounds you always.

May you grow in His care, walk in His light, and know that you are deeply loved today and every day.

Now Write Your Own Prayer

Did you know? God loves to hear *your* words, too!

Prayers don't have to rhyme or be long; they can be short, simple, and from your heart.

Here are some ideas to help you:

- "Thank You, God, for..."
- "Please help..."
- "I love You because..."

You can write, draw, or even just think your prayer. God hears it all.

My Prayer Today

My Prayer Today

Draw Your Prayer

Draw Your Prayer

Prayer for Someone I Love

Prayer for Someone I Love

Prayer for the World

Prayer for the World

Thank You, God

Thank You, God

My Night Prayer

My Night Prayer

AMEN

www.ingramcontent.com/pod-product-compliance
Lightning Source LLC
Chambersburg PA
CBHW061223070526
44584CB00029B/3955